Gazing Through Water

ALIFORM PUBLISHING

Minneapolis   Oaxaca

Acknowledgements

The translator and publisher would like to thank the editors of the following periodicals in which many of these poems first appeared, sometimes in slightly different versions:

Beltway Poetry Quarterly
Bitter Oleander
The Blue Nib
Burnside Review
Catamaran
Delos
Evansville Review
Faultline
The Fourth River
Great River Review
High Window
Lake Effect
Mantis
Metamorphoses
Moon City Review
The New York Times
Northwest Review
Osiris
Per Contra
Review: Literature and Arts of the Americas
Rock & Sling
Sirena
Solo

Praise for Astrid Cabral

On *Gazing Through Water*
In these new poems, masterfully translated by Alexis Levitin, Cabral faces her own mortality and the withering of body and spirit that comes with aging, offering us a poet's roadmap to a soul's preparation for death. The poems sing that limbo between acceptance of one's mortality and the "eagerness to survive," riffing back and forth between death and hope as a jazz musician might riff between major and minor keys. Those who love Cabral for her incandescent poetry celebrating nature will not be disappointed in this collection, as once again she looks to nature, especially her beloved Amazonia, for insight. At times philosophical, at times boldly physical and sensuous, she has knit a thread of impending darkness and loss throughout the poems. Still, moments of joy and, occasionally, wry humor abound; she can still celebrate "guava rosy" mornings, "sea syllables of salt and sun," and wish that "the passage be swift,/the hospital charges reasonable." If it is, as one of her poems suggests, a time of "small hopes," it is also a time to consider that final Garden she hopes to see, and of which these stunning, brave poems give us a glimpse.
Sheryl St. Germain, author of *Fifty Miles, How Heavy the Breath of God, Let It Be a Dark Roux*

What a gift to have such radiant poems from Astrid Cabral. And what a gift these translations from Alexis Levitin. The poems take us, quietly, into the deepest moments of mortality. And remind us, with grace, of immortality.
Mark Statman, author of *Exile/Home* and translator, with Pablo Medina, of Federico Garcia Lorca's *Poet in New York*

On her first book in English, *Cage*

I am so glad that Astrid Cabral's work has been brought together in Alexis Levitin's keen and knowing translation. Cabral has that wonderful variety that so many Brazilian poets have as she links together the threads of contemporary poetry in Brazil. Of particular interest are her descriptions of the creatures and plants of her native Amazonia, a region in need of the lyrical insight and home-grown sensibility shown here. Her work shows a marvelous range from traditional imagism to near concretism as she explores the panorama of Brazilian poetry.

Gregory Rabassa, translator of Clarice Lispector, Jorge Amado, and Joaquim Maria Machado de Assis, among other Brazilian writers

A keen awareness of how human beings and nature are irrevocably bound together... insightful observations about the beasts that lie within us...

Amy Elizabeth Fuller, *World Literature Today*

Cabral's poetry focuses not only on the simple beauty of nature; there is also a disturbing tone in her work about the destruction taking place there. Focusing primarily on the natural environment, Cabral's poems serve as reminders that human beings need take heed of their relationship to the earth. Levitin has done a remarkable job of preserving both these elements in translating Cabral's stunning poetic tribute to her native region, to her Cage of remembrance.

Enrica Ardemagni, Prof. Emerita of World Languages and Cultures, IUPUI

Gazing Through Water
Rasos d'água

by Astrid Cabral

Translated from the Portuguese by Alexis Levitin

ALIFORM PUBLISHING
aliformgroup@gmail.com
www.facebook.com/aliformpublishing

Aliform Publishing's editorial offices are
located at Earthquake Arts
San Pablo Etla, Oaxaca, México
Please direct all communication to aliformgroup@gmail.com
Aliform Publishing © 2021

Layout and design by Carolyn Borgen
Cover art by Laise de Sousa Varges

Set in Times New Roman

ISBN 9780982278499

Library of Congress Control Number: 2021941287

This is a print-on-demand book. Therefore, its country of
publication depends on the country in which the book was
purchased.

First edition of the English translation
Aliform Publishing

Table of Contents

Translator's Preface

In 2008 Host Publications brought out *Cage,* a collection of Amazonian poetry by Brazilian writer Astrid Cabral and her first book in English. After its publication, the poet and I embarked on a bilingual reading tour of the Northeast and the Midwest United States, often accompanying our presentations with a slide show on the Amazon. Heading home the day after our last presentation at Smith College in Massachusetts, we suddenly saw a sign for Walden Pond. We could not miss the opportunity to visit, for Astrid, one of Brazil's leading environmentalist poets, was in fact the translator of Thoreau's *Walden.*

Though evening was drawing near, we drove into the empty parking lot beside the lake as the sun began its descent from the sky. We wandered around in the thickening dusk, the remaining light gathered on the still surface of the water. As night fell, we lost the path and stumbled around in the darkness. Suddenly a powerful flashlight began moving towards us. It was a park ranger who, seeing our lone car, thought he would find wayward teenagers, not a couple of somewhat bewildered sexagenarians. Throughout this unplanned misadventure and indeed all of our travels, Astrid behaved with resilience and pluck, demonstrating the character that she acquired, no doubt, in her early years of intimacy with the Amazonian rainforest around her.

Astrid's infancy and childhood were spent in Manaus, the capital of Amazonas, and the Amazon has resonated throughout her life and throughout her poetry. Anyone who visits the jungle must be struck by the inescapable richness of its being, the heavy smells, the background chorus of insects and birds, the impenetrable barrier of green that lines all waterways, the endless sluggish flow of brown or black water wending towards the distant sea. Everywhere in the tropical forest resides the dialectic into which we all are plunged, the thriving symbiosis of two enormous pulsing, throbbing forces: the incessant fecundity of the life-force hidden in each crevice of the jungle's green wall, and the heavy smell of death that permeates everything. In the jungle and its waterways, life multiplies unceasingly, everywhere, in a frenzy of celebration. At the same time, it is accompanied by a frenzy of death all around, in the water, on the muddy shoreline, high in the branches of the overarching forest. Life and death, of course, are in unending combat wherever we go, but there is simply more of each, more birth, more creeping forth, more blossoming out, in the tropical forest, and more sudden death, more rot.

Cage was filled with a panoply of life forms drawn from memories of growing up in Amazonas. Perhaps the most salient vision was that of the pink river dolphin, the famed *bouto* of the Amazonian basin, one of only two species of freshwater dolphin in the world. Here is a brief poem, somehow realistic and surrealistic in its affirmation of the life-force.

"River Dolphin in the Body"
It flows in the depths of the body, a dark river
of muddied waters and deep desires
ancestral lymph midst furriness and urgency.
In it dwells a river dolphin, ready for the leap,
and it attacks so other rivers may be spawned
and life may not abort, but gush, gush forth, forever.

With this new volume in English, *Gazing Through Water,* Astrid Cabral confronts the personal imprint of time on herself and those around her. Having grown up on the banks of the greatest river on earth, she naturally sees time incarnated in the river's muddy flow, to which she returns again and again. At first the river, remembered, may appear in its fecundity, but later what dominates is its inexorable flow to the sea of oblivion, the universal death that awaits us all. Her river imagery, including smaller tributaries of the vast Amazon, depicts the external, environmental erosion and drought, with a dwindling of water and of life, while also speaking of her inner condition, as the vigor of her former youth diminishes, grows stagnant, runs dry. Accompanying the river's loss of life appear shadows of various other losses, the loss of childhood itself, of course, and the loss

2

of friends and colleagues. Then there is the slow struggle of her husband, as illness wears him down and he finally succumbs ("The Waiting Room" and "What is Lost."). But most sharp is the anguish of a mother at the sudden snuffing out of her young son's life in a car crash on the winding roads of the Atlantic Rainforest (such as "Tattoo," "The Other Face," "Sonnet," and "Encounter.") How to reconcile herself to the unbearable? And if not reconcile, then what?

In this collection from her mature, later years, we encounter the poet's struggle to go on in the face of despair. Clearly she stakes her claim for life on memory, memory and the word itself, as she wrestles against the total defeat of loss. This present volume, constructed from poems drawn from three collections, *Gazing Through Water, The Waiting Room,* and *Intimate Soot,* is her declaration of the poet's purpose in that uneven battle we all ultimately confront. With memory, she struggles to salvage the past, and with words she strives to give new substance to what has vanished from sight. For me, this book epitomizes the desperate glory of the poet's task: to cry out against the dark and somehow make that cry an affirmation.

Alexis Levitin
Morrisonville, NY   Spring, 2021

Part One:
Rasos d'agua / Gazing Through Water

To my son Giles,
presence and tears.

A meu filho Giles,
presença e pranto.

I washed my eyes
with many tears.
Now I see more clearly.

Lavei os olhos
em muitas lagrimas.
Agora vejo melhor.

Crepúsculo

Por que esta ânsia de sobreviver
assim se amoita no âmago de mim
sempre que as lerdas pálpebras da noite
baixam nas altas ramas com os morcegos?
Por que o poente assim me abala o eixo
e de fúnebre pompa alma me embrulha
tal qual mortalha um pouco prematura?
Por que me pesa suportar as trevas
que o implacável fim do dia instaura
quando já estagiei em precipícios
saltando trampolins perto de abismos?
Por que morrer me assusta e paralisa
se o que temo perder, de longe sei
nada tem de eldorado ou paraíso?

Twilight

Why does this eagerness to survive
hide like this deep in my core
whenever the sluggish eyelids of night
settle on the highest branches with the bats?
Why does the sunset shake my axis
and wrap my soul in funeral pomp
like a winding sheet, a little premature?
Why does it weigh on me to bear the darkness
the implacable end of day imposes
when I have already apprenticed in precipices
leaping from trampolines close by the abyss?
Why does the thought of dying frighten, paralyze me,
if what I fear to lose, I've known for so long now,
is far from Eldorado and from paradise?

De coração partido

O que me espanta
não é a morte
mas a vida, diga-se
a subvida da sobrevida.
O que me espanta
é a inércia do corpo
seu cego apetite
sob a alma inapetente.
O que me espanta
é o fôlego de fera
hibernando na crise
gelo sem primavera.
O que me espanta
é a resistência masoquista
que entre a ferida e o nada
do nada se acovarda
e resigna-se à ferida.

Broken Heart

What amazes me
isn't death
but life, that is to say
the half-life of life leftover.
What amazes me
is the inertia of the body
its blind appetite
beneath the apathetic soul.
What amazes me
is the breath of the beast
hibernating in the crisis
ice without spring.
What amazes me
is the masochistic resistance
that between pain and nothingness
grows faint-hearted before nothingness
and resigns itself to pain.

Vizinhança

Ao tocares o troféu
logo o brilho se azinhavra.
Seqüestrasses uma estrela
e terias entre os dedos
um arcabouço de lata.
Tira do castelo o amado
perderá coroa e cetro.
Melhor deixar o troféu
nas prateleiras do Olimpo.
Fique a estrela na galáxia.
Em nuvens se hospede o amado.
Qualquer vizinhança avilta
e apodrece os objetos.
Com o divino, o longínquo
tem parte. Só o impossível
partilha hálito celeste.

Familiarity

No sooner do you touch the trophy
than the brightness dims.
Seize a star
and you will find between your fingers
a skeleton of battered tin.
Take the beloved from the castle
both crown and scepter will be lost.
Better leave the trophy
on the shelves of Olympus.
Let the star stay in its galaxy.
And let the loved one dwell among the clouds.
Proximity defiles
familiarity corrupts all things.
With the divine, distance
plays its part. Only the impossible
partakes of the celestial breath.

O que se perde

Só o que está perdido é nosso para sempre.
Mário Quintana

Sombra espessa
onde se tropeça
ao meio-dia.
Cicatriz secreta
doendo na festa
sala vazia.
O que se perde
— não se perde —
reverte
zero onipresente.

What is Lost

Only what is lost is ours forever.
Mário Quintana

Thick shadow
where you flounder
at high noon.
Secret scar
throbbing at the party
the room a void.
What is lost
is not lost
it comes back--
an omnipresent zero.

Canção trôpega

A vida não tem volta.
Sobra o séquito de sombras
e uma canção trôpega
atravessada no peito:
espada, rubra espada
cravada de mau jeito.
Aqueles rapazes esbeltos
ai, estrangularam-se
nas gravatas da rotina.
Ai, crucificaram-se
no lenho das doenças.
Aqueles rapazes tão belos
não fazem mais acrobacias
nem discursos inflamados.
Arrastam chinelos e redes
ruminam silêncio amargo.
Um dia fui bela, filha,
digo a surpreendê-la.
Devo provar com retratos
o que tem ar de mentira.

Tottering Song

In life, there is no going back.
What's left is an entourage of shadows
and a tottering song
piercing the breast:
a sword, a blood-red sword
thrust in and stuck askew.
Those slim young guys
oh, how they got strangled
in the neckties of routine.
Oh, how they got crucified
on the cross-beams of disease.
Those guys, so handsome,
no longer do they do their acrobatic feats
or make a fervent speech.
Swaying back and forth in slippers and in hammocks
they ruminate the bitterness of silence.
Once upon a time, daughter, I was beautiful,
I say, surprising her.
I have to prove it with photos
for it sounds like a lie.

Metamorfose

Ainda nos chamam
pelos mesmos nomes.
Acaso seremos os mesmos
ou é a cegueira alheia?
Éramos formosos
afortunados donos
de sesmarias de sonhos.
Tínhamos frescor de frondes
ímpetos de fontes e fogos
destemor de duelos, dúvidas
que não machucavam quase.
Éramos potros selvagens
farejando precipícios
pelas pastagens do mundo.
No curral ainda nos sobra
a noção do tesouro perdido
e essa ração de memória
é a esmola que nos cabe.

Metamorphosis

They still call us by the same names.
Could it be we are the same,
or are the others blind?
We were lovely looking
lucky lords
of extended lands of dreams.
We had the freshness of fronds
the force of fountains and of flames
the dauntlessness of duels, doubts
that almost didn't hurt.
We were wild ponies
grazing the precipices
of the pastures of the world.
In the corral we still retain
a notion of the treasure we have lost
and that ration of memory
is the alms that still belong to us.

Terceira idade

Poupem palavras panos mornos.
Minados fracos os ossos
cabelos ralos desbotados.
No sorriso algumas falhas
navalhas muitas na alma.
Nos órgãos sinais de falência
e a dependência se inicia:
médicos drogas e drágeas.
Por favor não falem de
maturidade e sabedoria.
Pois de que valeriam
atrasadas, sem serventia,
na instância de sufoco
do corpo em atrofia?
Nada de pseudoconsolos.
Por que tapar com peneira
as muitas perdas e danos?
Então será caridade
mascarar a subtração?

The Golden Years

Enough of all that phony stuff.
The bones are riddled, undermined,
hair thinned, lack-luster, dull.
In the smile some things missing
and in the soul a dagger.
In the organs signs of failure and decay
the end of independence on its way:
doctors drugs the doling out of pills.
Please don't speak
of wisdom and maturity
for what's the point when they will be
arriving useless and quite late,
just as the body, atrophied,
begins at last to suffocate?
No pseudo-consolation.
Why play blindman's buff
with the losses and the pain?
Would that be charity in action
to mask the process of subtraction?

Áureos tempos

Áureos tempos aqueles
quando na manhãzinha goiaba
colhíamos no cerrado *gabirobas*
ainda vestidas de orvalho.
Pés e patas competiam no capim
pródigo de carrapichos.
Gestos elásticos ultra-rápidos
assustávamos insetos e aves.
Um séquito de suaves súditos
nos seguia em semi-adoração
nós, os príncipes daquele feudo.
Depois, o asfalto rasgou o campo.
Cogumelos de concreto brotaram.
Cresceram as crianças e a cidade.
Anãs ficaram as árvores aos pés
de edifícios colossais. Sumiram
pássaros *gabirobas* araçás.
Fim de passeios e piqueniques.
Só ficou a fome funda das frutas
no vão sem remissão das bocas.

Youth

Those were golden days
when early in the guava-rosy morning
we gathered in the open fields gabiroba fruit
still bathed in dew.
Feet and paws scrambled through
the thistled grass.
With elastic gestures, frantic fast,
we startled birds and insects.
A procession of faithful vassals
followed us in semi-adoration,
us, the princelings of that feudal realm.
Later, asphalt tore apart the field.
Concrete mushrooms sprouted forth.
The city and the children grew.
Trees turned to dwarves at the foot
of colossal buildings. Birds,
gabirobas, wild guavas disappeared.
The end of pleasant wanderings and picnics.
All that remained was the craving for those fruit
in the unforgiving emptiness of our mouths.

Cemitério líquido

Ao rolar de pardos dias
até o choro convulso
tornou-se morno sereno.
Lâminas cegas não mais
ceifam emoções aos feixes.
Na carne em salmoura imersa
os ímpetos hoje murchos
exibem talos pendidos.
O que era clamor de mar
vagas de marés, procelas
fez-se lago surdo-mudo
ou um cemitério líquido.
Os vulcões já serenados
soterram outras pompéias
e o hábito, tão-só o hábito
é a corda que lhe gira
os rasos gestos em que
gasta o restante dos dias.

Liquid Cemetery

As the drab days roll by
even the convulsive sobs
subside to lukewarm quietude.
Blind blades no longer
scythe emotions into bundles.
In flesh immersed in brine
impulses withered now
expose their drooping stems.
What was the roaring of the waves,
the swelling of the tides, tempests at sea,
have become a deaf-mute pond,
a liquid cemetery.
Volcanoes now calm
hide other Pompeys,
and habit, just habit,
is the spring that moves
those shallow gestures in which she spends
the remainder of her days.

Cenário antigo

O oitizeiro junto ao muro
cresceu somente um pouco.
No portão há mais ferrugem
e a casa abrigou o musgo
além das rugas lavradas
sob o terçado das chuvas.
A rigor, nada mudou.
Mas onde as palavras ternas
(que supunha eternas)
as carícias ainda tímidas
o êxtase das descobertas?
É como se tudo houvesse
escorrido pelo ralo
e o vivido não passasse
de sonho ou imaginação.
Foste embora e ora retornas
feito alma penada, igual
àquelas que rondavam
o meu pavor de criança.
Digo pois, "xô, xô, saudade"
não mais de ti, de mim
botão aberto sob afagos.
Junto ao muro, descubro então:
coração não é só músculo.
É sobretudo sarcófago.

Ancient Scenario

The *outizeiro* tree beside the wall
has only grown a bit.
There is more rust on the gate
and the house has gathered moss
along with streaks carved
by the plowshare of the rains.
In fact, nothing has changed.
 But where are the tender words
(I thought eternal)
the caresses still timid
the ecstasy of discovery?
It is as if everything has
gone down the drain
and what we lived was nothing
but a dream or imagining.
You went away and now come back
like an afflicted soul,
one of those that prowled
the terrors of my childhood.
And so I say, shoo shoo, nostalgia,
no more of you, of me,
bud blossoming beneath caresses.
Beside that wall, I now discover:
the heart is not mere muscle.
More than anything, it is a sepulcher.

A casa no breu

Faz tanto tempo
que deixei aquela casa.
Confesso: não sei mais
da estrada nem da chave.
É como se ficasse em cidade
sem nome, em outro planeta
ou nem existisse mais.
No entanto não sei como
de vez em quando algo
me arrebata e me arrasta
ao seu regaço de breu.
Tudo o que ouço é o vôo cego
dos morcegos no vão das telhas
e uma torneira pingando
  sem parar.
Será o choro de minha mãe na sala
ou serei eu mesma em pranto?

House Pitch-Black

I left that house
so long ago.
I confess: I know nothing now of
the road and of the key.
It's as if it stayed behind in a nameless
city, on another planet,
or simply ceased to exist.

Nonetheless, I don't know how
once in a while something
catches hold and draws
me back to its pitch-black breast.
All I hear is the blind flight
of bats beneath the rooftop
and a faucet dripping
        endlessly.

Could it be my mother crying in the living room,
or could it be myself in tears?

Cinzas na Guanabara

Para Helena Ferreira

De leve toco na pele
do mar a tez de Clotilde.
Sinto na orla da espuma
despido de cor ou som
seu sorriso a se afogar.
Adivinho-lhe nas vagas
o volume frio das mãos
o corpo que me abraçava.
Quem na terra foi compacta
presença, sutil passeia
agora em campinas d'água
dorme elíptica na areia
cabelos presos em algas.
A figura tão visível
— escondida para sempre
na mortalha azul sem fim —
do mar da lembrança emerge.

Ashes in Guanabara

for Helena Ferreira

Lightly I touch on the surface
of the sea Clotilde's skin.
I feel along the fringes of the foam,
stripped of color and of sound,
her smile drowning.
I sense among the waves
the cold volume of her hands,
the body that embraced me.
What on earth was compact
presence, now strolls tenuous
through watery fields,
sleeps elliptical in the sand,
seaweed tangled in her hair.
Her monumental figure
--hidden now forever
in the endless winding sheet of blue-
emerges from the sea of memory.

Mudança

Evaporaram com ela
a alfazema na alcova
e a canela na sobremesa.
Juntos sumiram o brilho
de alfaias espelhos vidros
murmúrio de pés no chão
cochicho de mãos em bilros.
Resta o tremor das avencas
no alpendre abandonado
e o trinado dos canários
no amanhecer do quintal.
Não adianta procurá-la
na lápide do subúrbio longe.
Ela nunca esteve mais perto
ancorada de vez em teu peito.

Change

Lavender in the alcove
cinnamon at breakfast
evaporating along with her.
They vanished all together, the glint
of ornaments mirrors windows
the murmur of feet across the floor
the whisper of hands at bobbins.
What now remains is the trembling of maidenhair
on the abandoned porch
and the trilling of canaries
in the backyard break of day.
No use seeking her
beneath a gravestone in a distant suburb.
She has never been closer,
anchored now forever in your breast.

Tatuagem

Em mim esta indelével tatuagem:
não mera mancha, nódoa em tela ou derme
na alma, porém, em sua oculta carne.
Não com as longínquas tintas do Pacífico
mas com os sombrios tons do que é tragédia.
Há um verde de ramos desmaiados
preto piche de noite desestrelada
um vermelho a pender para o tom roxo:
sangue sustado no fluxo do corpo.
Vê-se uma árvore que se contorce
sob o brutal impacto de um carro
enquanto os deuses arrebatam um jovem.

Tattoo

An indelible tattoo in me:
no simple spot, no stain on cloth or skin
but on the soul, that hidden flesh.
Not made with far Pacific tints
but with the sombre tones of tragedy.
There is a fainting green of branches
the pitch-black blackness of a starless night
red bleeding into amaranth:
blood suspended in the body's flux.
Look how a tree contorts
from the brutal impact of a car
as the gods snatch up another youth.

Quem?

Quem poderia dizer
porque atravessaste o rio
quando na margem de cá
havia frondes e sombras
flores em todo esplendor?
Mãos e ramos te acenavam
e o canto de muitas gargantas
embalava teus ouvidos.
Que ousadia ou medo
te levou ao outro lado?
Sobraram botas sandálias
e a dor desse segredo
machucando feito dardo.
Sei, não tens mais voz
para qualquer resposta.
Ó deuses surdos-mudos
        quem, senão vós,
nos revelaria tudo?

Who?

Who could say
why you crossed the river
when on this bank
there was leafy foliage and shade
and flowers in full splendour?
Hands and branches waved to you
and a song from many throats
lulled your ears.
What daring or what fear
led you to the other side?
You've left behind your boots and sandals
and the pain of that secret
stabbing like a spear.
I know, you have no voice
with which to answer anymore.

Oh, deaf-mute gods,
    who, if not you,
will unveil at last all things to us.

Soneto

Junto a mim decorreu a tua vida
no curto tempo em que fui tua casa.
Paredes de osso e carne eram guarida
quando no sono o ser desabrochavas.
Do amor à sombra e posto a meu cuidado
em tantas terras e sob tantos tetos
a espalhar alegria em todo lado
preso estavas nas redes de um afeto.
Se de mim te afastavas te seguia
adivinhando aflita a tua trilha
até no emaranhado mapa vê-la
a esperar, a esperar que em algum dia
retornasses, atrás deixando a ilha.
Teu endereço agora é nas estrelas.

Sonnet

In that short time when I was still your home,
inside, attached to me, your life unrolled.
Your sanctuary was of flesh and bone
and there I felt your sleeping soul unfold.

Shaded by my love, given to my care,
beneath so many roofs, in different lands,
you radiated joy, your gift to share,
while caught up in the weave of loving hands.

If you would leave me, I would follow you
guessing, distressed, which way you must have gone,
till in the tangled map your path would clear

while I would wait and wait in hope of news
of you, come back to here where you belong.
Your home is now among the stars and spheres.

Hokusai e a grande onda

Hokusai disse à onda:
Aquieta-te, inquieta.
Égua d'água detém
no ar o impulso das patas.
Quero-te estátua eqüestre
as crinas de cristal.
Mãos de deus, Hokusai
bota o tempo nas grades
logra o triunfo da arte.
Tinta e papel em vagas
rebolam celebrando
a proeza pelas praias.
Devorador de troféus,
o mar segue zombando:
Oh presunção utópica!
Oh ilusão de ótica!
Cedo ou tarde, ele engole
os inúteis papéis.

Hokusai and the Great Wave

Hokusai said to the wave:
quiet down, unquiet one.
Watery mare, restrain
your pawing thrust of hooves in air.
I want you to be an equestrian statue
with a crystal mane.

With the hands of a God, Hokusai
places time behind bars
achieving the triumph of art.
Ink and paper tumble
in waves celebrating
his prowess all along the beach.

Devourer of trophies,
the sea goes on with its derision:
Oh, utopian presumption!
Oh, optical illusion!
Sooner or later, it will swallow up
these useless sheets of paper.

Mar incansável mar

Mar incansável mar
    eterno a murmurar
        sílabas de sol e sal
mar a embalar
    molhadas multidões
        vôos implumes de cardumes
manadas de mamíferos marinhos
    polvos   lulas   conchas   crustáceos
matas de corais e moitas de algas
        a desabrochar e a dançar
            em covas e cavas
mar a se espraiar
    em litorais de rasas praias
        rendas de restingas
mar a se chocar em cascos
            de altos penhascos
        escarpas de costas brutas
mar incansável motor
        a multiplicar espumas
            rápidas dunas d'água
lombadas
    lambadas   bolhas trás bolhas
        ondas trás ondas
mar órgão colossal a gerar
    sons   sílabas   sussurros   urros
mar pasto de mistérios
    insolúveis no azul
        translúcido ou noturno
mar cemitério
    velas   caravelas   âncoras
        ossos   destroços
            ferros-velhos
mar de mudas falas
    significados de silêncios

Sea, Tireless Sea

Sea, tireless sea
    murmuring eternity
        of syllables of salt and sun
Sea rocking
    watery multitudes
        unfeathered schools in flight
masses of marine mammals
    octopuses   squid   conch   cuttlefish
forests of coral and fronds of algae
        branching and dancing
            in sea caves and in coves
sea spreading over
    endless level sands
        or lace worked strips and spits of land
sea beating at the hulk
        of towering cliffs
        and bulking slopes of savage coasts
sea tireless engine
        churning its spume
            its rapid watery dunes
its roiling crashing
    slashing crests   bubble after bubble
        wave after wave
sea colossal organ generating
    sounds   syllables   susurrations   ululations
sea pasture of insoluble
    mysteries in blue
        translucent or nocturnal
maritime cemetery
    tattered sails   battered caravels   anchors
        bones stones   flotsam jetsam
            rusting wreckage
sea of unspoken speech
    significance of silences

mar música pura

mar   saliva   suor   pranto

de um arcaico deus oculto.

sea of utter music
sea   saliva   sweat   tears
of an ancient hidden god.

O azul assassino

O mar, o mar, oh deleite,
atravesso-lhe montanhas
e morros como se fossem de azeite.
Na pele o líquido luar
e a saliva sal das vagas.
Contudo eis que chegam a mim
sujo e ferrugem de quilhas
relíquias de sonhos a pique
sobras de mastros e velas
restos de monstros, de vidas.
Tudo escondido nas dobras
cheias de sombra, sem lume
do imenso azul assassino.
Lembrem-se apenas cardumes.

Blue Assassin

The sea, the sea, oh what unspoken joy,
I cross its mounds
and mountains as if they were of oil.
On its skin liquid moonlight
and the salt saliva of its waves.
And yet behold what comes to me:
filth and the rust of keels
relics of dreams gone down
debris of masts and sails
remains of monsters and of lives.
And all lie hidden from the light
in the shadow-filled folds
of that abysmal blue assassin.

May fish alone school our remembered nights.

Águas e conchas

Sem debrum, os sonhos dançam
apagando os perfis de espuma
na crista imprevista das ondas.
Definidas, as lembranças
cabem nas mãos feito conchas
pedras de cascos e quinas
estátuas de sal saídas
do mar — água indefinida.

Water and Shells

Without pleats, dreams dance
extinguishing silhouettes of spume
on unexpected crests of waves.
Memories, defined,
fit in my hands like shells
bits of hulls and keels
statues of salt come
from the sea—its waters undefined.

Três pingos

A chuva
clandestina
pela rua
madrugava.
A chuva
neblina
xixi de jia
me molhava.
A chuva
magrinha
luva de veludo
me calçava.

Three Drops

Rain
softly sifts
the street,
its dawning gray.

Rain
a mist
of frog piss.
A deep, damp day.

Rain
drops drift
a velvet glove
upon my human clay.

O rio de antanho

Para Aída e Dirceu Costa

Sangue na carne da terra
aquele rio em surdina
molhava-me os pés e a alma
de quando eu era menina.
Amanhecia comigo
embrulhado pelos xales
da mais branca cerração
e comigo anoitecia
embalado por cantigas
de mil mosquitos e grilos.
Ninguém a mim perguntasse
pelo berço do caudal
ou o endereço da corrente.
Para mim fosse redondo
seu deslizar de serpente.
Levando a face do tempo
na pele marrom do lombo
não passava de morada
de estrelas cardumes luas
espelho de lindas nuvens
cama onde o sol se deitava.
Nos meandros da lembrança
aquele rio de antanho
taciturno estagnou-se.
Virou poça, água de tina
bacia onde me banho.

River of Yesteryear

For Aida and Dirceu Costa

Blood on the flesh of the earth
that muted river
would wet my feet and soul
when I was a child.
It would dawn with me
wrapped in shawls
of the whitest mist
and it would set with me
lulled by the singing
of mosquitoes and a thousand crickets.
It would have been in vain to ask me
of the current's cradle
or of the torrent's course.
For me its serpent slither
was a rounded whole.
Carrying the face of time
on its chestnut-colored back
it was just the dwelling place
of stars schools of fish moons
mirror to lovely clouds
bed where the sun would lie down.
In the meanderings of memory
that silent river of
yesteryear ceased to flow.
It turned into a pool, a tub,
a basin where I take my bath.

Ex-rio

Aqui jaz um rego.
Por aqui passava um rio
faz trinta anos.
Quem bebeu o rio?
De quem tamanha sede?
Entre pedras e areias
restam resíduos de vida.
Mas onde nas margens pardas
as digitais dos assassinos?

Ex-river

Here lies a ditch;
thirty years ago
a river passed through here.

Who drank the river?
Who suffered such a thirst?

Between the stones and sands
mere vestiges of life remain.

But where along these darkened banks
are the killer's fingerprints?

Primeiro espelho

A flor das águas
foi o primeiro espelho do universo.
Nele, as nuvens
descobriram seu perfil de plumas
e assistiram à própria coreografia
sob a batuta dos ventos.
Já o firmamento
acorrentado ao feitiço
de constelações e luas duplicadas
foi o precursor de Narciso.

First Mirror

The surface of the waters
was the first mirror of the universe.

In it, the clouds
discovered their feathery forms
and were present at their own choreography
beneath the wind's baton.

Even then the firmament
fettered to the magic of
constellations and repeating moons
was precursor to Narcissus.

Viagem à revelia

Se por enquanto deslizo
pelas espáduas do rio
e mal lhe distingo as margens
se tudo agora ignoro
sobre a fonte ou mesmo a foz
salvo a aresta da pergunta
que o peito me dilacera
se por enquanto me visto
com lantejoulas de sol
ou às vezes me descubro
órfã no luto da noite
uma lição aprendi:
devo apascentar as ondas
e louvar a companhia
que me faz a própria sombra
na viagem à revelia.

Unwilling Journey

If for the time being I glide
along the river's shoulder
and scarcely can discern its banks
if I know nothing now
about its source or even where it ends
except for the sharp-honed question
that lacerates my breast
if for the time being I see myself
with sequins of sunshine
or sometimes find myself
an orphan in night's mourning
one lesson I have learned:
I have to calm the waves
and praise the company
that my own shadow casts
on this unwilling journey.

Escalas

Imenso, o navio me ultrapassa.
O passo miúdo não alcança proa nem popa.
Ao pequeno olhar, afrontado
pela extensão do horizonte em volta,
sobra a sensação de ilha móvel, o embalo.
Eu, à cintura de altos vultos, junto
à mãe embrulhada em luto e choro.
Os avós me dizem, vais trocar o mar azul
pelo Rio Negro. Vais morar em Manaus.
Mãos fortes me conduzem ao longo
do convés oscilando entre azuis
na gangorra de nuvens e de ondas.
Mar, mar, por todos os lados, no olho
redondo e esbugalhado de todas as vigias.
Segurando as cordas de esguia escada
deixo para trás Recife, a casa com pombos
o tamarineiro ao fim do beco, praias,
bichos e vozes familiares e entro
no estranho universo do vapor: apitos,
máquinas e motores ronronando,
cheiros de tinta, zarcão, pinho, sabão
maresias, o vento gelando-me dedos e nariz,
salões, corredores, camarotes, degraus
e no convés, o mar emoldurando o mundo
enquanto as horas se espicham compridas
espremidas entre auroras e crepúsculos,
luares e olhos cintilantes no breu marinho
até que desembarco em Belém e avisto
o porto constelado de barcos mastros velas.
Pessoas desconhecidas me acolhem
e me levam sob um dossel de folhas
por terra firme onde se arrastam
sobre as pedras da rua, vastas tartarugas
de metal, os vagarosos automóveis.

Scales-of-Call

Immense, the ship beyond my reach.
My toddling step cannot get to prow or stern.
In my little gaze, confronted
by horizon all around,
just the feeling of an island, rocking.
I, to the waist of tall shapes, beside
my mother wrapped in mourning and in tears.
My grandparents told me, you're going to trade the blue sea
for the Rio Negro. You're going to live in Manaus.
Strong hands led me along
the deck rocking between two blues
a seesawing of clouds and waves.
Sea, sea, on all sides sea, in all
the round and bulging porthole eyes.
Clinging to the gangplank ropes
I leave Recife behind, the house with pigeons
the tamarind tree at the end of the alley, beaches,
animals and familiar voices and enter
the strange universe of the steamship: whistles,
machinery and engines purring,
the smell of paint, cinnabar, pinewood, soap,
sea salt air, wind freezing my fingers and my nose,
ballrooms, corridors, cabins, steps
and, on deck, the sea framing the world
while the hours stretch out endless
interlaid with dawns and dusks,
and moonlight and eyes glistening in ocean dark
till disembarking in Belém I see
the port spangled with boats masts sails.
Unknown people greet me
and on terra firma bring me
beneath a canopy of leaves to where enormous
metal tortoises crawl along
the cobbled streets, lumbering automobiles.

Caminho rés da parede crespa
e me defronto com ampla vitrine
reluzente de verniz e altos vidros.
E eis que ali, mínimo como eu mesma,
ancora, divino, um navio de brinquedo
maquete dos gaiolas que singram
o dorso de rios, igarapés, paranás.
Enfim, o meu olhar o abarca. Enfim aterrisso
reconciliada com minha dimensão.
Quero intensamente tocá-lo, ingressar
em seu espaço, inserir-me nele.
Porém dali me arrastam. Choro embargado,
volto à solidão do oceano horas a fio.
Fico a ver navios, a ver navios
enquanto o mar me leva ao rio.

I walk close to the rough wall
and soon am facing a great shop window
glistening with varnish and high panes.
And behold, there, as small as I myself,
a model ship, divine, is anchored,
a replica of the steamer's sailing
the backs of rivers, channels, a distant reach.
Finally my gaze could take it in. Finally I come to land
reconciled to my dimensions.
I intensely wish to touch it, enter
its space, insert myself in it.
However, they drag me away from there. Stymied, I cry.
I return to ocean solitude, hours on end.
I stand there watching bubbles burst, bubbles burst,
as the sea bears me off to where the river wends.

Recife no fundo do poço

As raízes da alegria
remontam a ruas de pedra
nuvens nadando riachos.
São cúmplices de junquilhos
tamarindos, galos e grilos
arautos de lua e sol.
Elas se enredam nos pés
molhados de sal e no ar
onde voei em ave de aço.
Pela memória do pai
a perdida alegria
renasce e acende o dia.

Recife at the Bottom of the Well

Roots of joy
climb again those streets of stone
clouds swimming in the tiny streams.

They are partners to jonquils
tamarinds, cockerels and crickets
heralds of the moon and sun.

They envelop my feet
wet with salt and the air
where once I rode a bird of steel.

Through the memory of my father
the lost joy
is born again and lights the day.

Águas do Tapajós

Ó águas do Tapajós,
quantas vezes adiei
os convites de viagem?
Quantos amores joguei
nesse regaço de jade?
Ó águas do Tapajós,
não sois as mesmas de outrora
nem sou eu a mesma de antes.
Hoje em vós navego o ser
órfão incorpóreo de fé
e qualquer sonho de porto.
(Os portos também são cárceres)
Ó águas do Tapajós,
o verde de vossa pele
já se tinge de nanquim.
A tarde tornou-se noite
e é tão tarde que não cabe
qualquer pausa pelas margens.
(Santarém, estás bem longe
já não te alcançam meus remos)
Ó Tapajós, entanguida
de dor, rendo-me à deriva
do fundo líquido jade.
Ó águas do Tapajós,
nosso rumo é mesmo a foz.

Waters of the Tapajós

Oh, waters of the Tapajós,
how often did I put off
your invitations?
How many loves did I toss away
into your lap of jade?
Oh, waters of the Tapajós,
you aren't the same as once you were
nor am I the same as way back when.
Today my being sails in you
incorporeal orphan of faith
and any dreamed of port.
(Ports, too, are prisons)
Oh, waters of the Tapajós,
the green of your skin
is turning now to India ink.
Afternoon has turned to night
and now it is too late
for any pause along the banks.
(Santarém, you are far away
my oars no longer reach you)
Oh, Tapajós, numb
with pain, I give myself
to your jade deep liquid flow.
Oh, waters of the Tapajós,
we are set for the river's mouth.

Chafariz

Chafariz:
cambalhota de chuva
em almofariz de pedra.
Cascata sem rebeldia
águas disciplinadas
bailando a céu aberto.
Riacho relinchando
líquidas crinas
no dia em chama.

Fountain

Fountain:
somersault of rain
in a mortar of stone.

Cascade without revolt
disciplined waters
dancing beneath an open sky.

Rivulet's nicker
liquid mane
on a day in flames.

Calamidade

Águas na sala! Peixes nos quartos!
Quem entenderia?
Degredados das paisagens
contidos em urbanas grades
eles encharcavam
não só os chinelos de lama
a alma também de espanto.
Todos esquecidos
dos troncos derrubados
dos leitos rasos – antepassados
das chuvas dilúvio.

Calamity

Water in the hallway! Fish in the bedroom!
Who could understand it all?
Exiled from the countryside
confined within an urban grid
not just their slippers
soaked in mud,
but their souls in fright.
Everyone oblivious
to the demolished trees
the silted riverbeds—forefathers
to the diluvial flood.

Rio paralítico

Rios percorrem-me infinitos
pelas areias da lembrança.
Manchas de luz som e frescor
irrigando o solo da alma.
Passam em fundo de quintal
vasculares ciscando o chão
como quem pede passagem
ou trazem o ímpeto audaz
de correntezas e saltos.
Todos são irmãos do tempo
que jamais se detém
todos a imagem da vida
na aflita sina do sangue.
Este rio paralítico me assusta:
pausa de gelo, cadáver exposto
morte ao alcance dos dedos.

Paralytic River

Streams flow through me infinite
across the sands of memory.
Patches of light sound and freshness
watering the soil of the soul.
Vascular, they pass along far
down the yard sweeping trash away
but timidly, as if abashed
or boldly splash, brash with the force
of rapids and of waterfalls.
All are brothers to time
that never lingers
all images of life
the doom of our afflicted blood.

This paralytic river frightens me:
the immobility of ice, the corpse exposed
death at our fingertips.

Acimabaixo

Longe fica a fonte.
Alcançá-la
é cruzar
águas contrárias.
Perto fica a foz.
Atingi-la
é deitar-se
à deriva veloz.

Abovebelow

The fountainhead is far away.
To reach it
is to go
against the river's flow.

The river's mouth is close.
To get there
just lie down
and swiftly drift the way the river goes.

Part Two:
Ante-sala / Waiting Room

*One is always in the dark, only at the
last last do they flood the room with light.*
Guimarães Rosa
Bedevilled in the Badlands

*Um está sempre no escuro, só no último
derradeiro é que clareiam a sala.*
Guimarães Rosa
Grande sertão: veredas

Ante-sala

Este o mundo
de mistérios
refratários
a microscópios.

Este o mundo
de muralhas
inexpugnáveis
a máquinas.

Aqui a noite
opaca e parca
de estrelas.

Aqui os olhos
embrulhados
em dobras e sombras.

Esta a ante-sala:
áspera espera
de outra era.

Waiting Room

Here a world
of mysteries
immune
to microscopes.

Here a world
of walls
no machine can breach.

Here a night
opaque and spare
of stars.

Here eyes
enclosed
in folds and shadows.

Here a waiting room:
the bitter weight as we await
our fate.

Grades

Assim, embalando a linda
ilusão da liberdade
foges, corres e te evades.
Rejeitas o chão dos montes
que te atrapalha a passagem.
Queres o longe horizonte
onde terra e céu se casem.
As asas do sonho aos ombros
vais de cidade em cidade
casa em casa, loja em loja.
Quebras ferrolhos e portas.
Rompes cadeados e chaves.
Inútil qualquer esforço.
Nunca te sentirás livre.
Vê: por toda parte há grades.

Bars

And so, rocking in your arms the lovely
dream of liberty,
you run away, fleeing from yourself.
You reject the jagged ground
that blocks your way.
You yearn for far horizons
where earth and sky come together.
The wings of dream at your shoulders
you go from city to city
house to house, store to store.
You break through bolts, burst open doors,
tear padlocks apart, snap keys in half.
All your efforts are in vain.
You will never feel that you are free.
Look around: barred windows everywhere.

Entre Jardins

Sobre a calçada, paineiras
desmoronam a primavera.

No lixo pistilos juntam-
se a alvos cabelos caídos.

Murcho debaixo de chuvas
assassinada por luas.

Em mim, porém, reina a fé:
noutro jardim vou nascer.

Envergarei outras cores
em nova forma de ser.

Between Gardens

On the sidewalk, silk-cotton trees
undo the spring.

In the garbage pistils mix
with grizzled fallen hairs.

I wither beneath the rains
murdered by the moon.

And yet, faith reigns in me:
I will be born into another garden.

I will clothe myself in other colors
in another form of being.

Transitória

Enquanto

                folhas folham
                árvores arvoram
                e o dia irradia

sigo
    figo

                no ramo da tarde.

Até que a noite anoiteça
o fruto apodreça
e na terra em fome

                          tombe

sem alarde.

Ephemeral

While
              foliage unfolds
              trees turn to trees
              and day dazzles
I still cling
   a fig
              on a sprig of afternoon.

Till day's dust dusks
fruit rots
              then drops
to the hungry earth
without a fuss.

Subterrânea

Os tempos de rio passaram.
Sou montanha impassível:
a roupa das estações
de leve me aflora a pele.
O eterno é que me veste.

Underground

The river's moods have passed.
I am an unmoved mountain:
the seasons' clothes
lightly brush my flesh.
Eternity is now my dress.

Morros e cogumelos

Os morros não morrem.
Omoplatas e espáduas
de granito calcário ferro
contemplam soberanos
o inquieto barro dos homens
esses breves cogumelos
brotando e mergulhando
séculos após séculos
nos troncos da terra.

Hills and Mushrooms

Hills don't die.
Sloping shoulder blades
of granite limestone iron
they contemplate as sovereigns
the restless clay of humankind
those brief mushrooms
sprouting forth and drooping down
century after century
on the trunks of the earth.

Invisíveis

Mortos evaporaremos
e seremos invisíveis
tal e qual a cor dos *quarks*
a mola atrás dos milagres
a chave-mor dos mistérios
os dedos de Deus nos céus.

Invisible

Dead we will evaporate
and be invisible
just like the color of quarks
the mechanism of miracles
the master key to mysteries
God's fingers in the heavens.

No colo do anjo

Empoleirado
na torre do meu sonho
um anjo resplandece.

Cílios cintilantes
estrelas nos olhos
ele me acena com plumas
e me abraça com asas.

Juntos vagamos
entre rastros de astros
a cavalgar nuvens
por planícies etéreas
até que me sinto serena.

É como se mudo dissera
não temas véus ou névoas
qualquer neblina passa.
Mas eis que então fala:

Não sejas cega, menina.
O olhar de Deus tudo abarca.
Só os homens têm pálpebras.

In the Angel's Embrace

Perched
on the tower of my dream
an angel gleams.

Scintillating lashes
stars in his eyes
he beckons me with feathers
and embraces me with wings.

Together we wander
arching trails of stars
riding on clouds
across ethereal plains
until I feel at peace.

It is as if he had silently said
fear neither veils nor haze
all mists will pass away.
But see what he says then:

Child, don't be blind.
The gaze of God embraces everything.
Only humankind have eyelids on their eyes.

Herança

Bênçãos e maldições vêm de bem longe
embaladas em ovos, sangue e esperma
em arquivos que jazem sob a terra
lacrados, chaves já perdidas no ontem.
Os vivos farejamos crus mistérios
e giramos perguntas parafusos
que mal roçam a cútis dos arcanos:
o olhar terá nascido no jurássico?
o tom de tez e voz será adâmico?
de quem decorre esta imprevista herança
de sermos o que bem ou mal nós somos?
Família, amor, jogo de sexo e espelhos
por onde assim perplexos nos lançamos
ou, dizendo melhor, lançados fomos.

Legacy

Blessings and curses come from blood
and sperm, wrapped up long ago in eggs,
in archives that lie sealed beneath
the earth, keys lost long ago.
The living, we sniff at naked mysteries
and turn the screws of questions
that barely graze the skin of the arcane:
was our gaze born in the Jurassic?
is the color of our skin and voice Adamic?
from whom does it unfold, this unexpected legacy
of being what, for good or ill, we are?
Family, love, the play of sex and mirrors
into which bewildered we throw ourselves
or, better yet, are thrown.

A cara da morte

Quando a vertigem do sono
deitou-me em vale de sombras
de relance te vi nu
correndo ao tanque das águas.

Só mais tarde, ao despertar
tua ausência me assombrou.
Precipitei-me água adentro.
Onde estás, menino afoito?

Então sob um cobertor
de fundas águas azuis
te vi deitado sereno
em duro chão de azulejo.

Consegui chegar à tona
pondo-te nos ombros qual
homem da Emulsão de Scott,
com seu peixe morto às costas.

Mas não eras um cadáver!
Deus! teu coração batia
suave, teu pulmão arfava
em meio ao rumor das águas.

Pude, enfim, nesse mergulho
de cara encarar a morte:
ela não é força que amor
mate ou de vez nos aparte.

The Face of Death

When the vertigo of sleep
left me in the valley of the shadow
suddenly I saw you naked
running to the water tank.

Only later, waking up,
did your absence strike me.
I threw myself into the water.
Where are you, heedless child?

And then, beneath the deep
blue water blanket
I see you lying peacefully
on the hard-tiled bottom of the pool.

I manage to reach the surface
with you on my shoulders
like that man in the ad,
bearing a dead fish on his back.

But you were not a corpse!
God! Your heart was beating
softly, your lungs were heaving
in the middle of the murmur of the water.

And so, in that dive, I could,
at last, confront death face to face:
it's not a force that can kill love
or keep us separate forever.

Do outro lado

A quilômetros do abismo
tranqüilo,o recém defunto
de grinaldas coroado
toma chá com torradas
celebrando a travessia
pelo espelho metafísico.

From the Other Side

Miles away from the abyss,
crowned with garlands,
someone calm and freshly dead
is taking tea and toast
celebrating having crossed
the mirror and its metaphysics.

Receita

Jamais desceu às raízes.
Ficou sempre pelas ramas.
Por isso é que ele sorri
e seu corpo vive em dança.
Trouxe a receita consigo:
a terra sólida trava
enquanto o ar macio embala.

Recipe

He never went down to the roots,
but always clung to the branches.
That's why he's smiling
and his body lives a dance.
He brought his recipe along with him:
solid earth's a shackle,
soft air a lullaby.

O precário olhar

A retina não alcança
o que escondido se trama.
Sequer adivinha o tato
o que além da pele cresce.
Lentes e lupas não suprem
a congênita cegueira.
Ficamos sempre aquém
da nítida linha onde o ouro
de um pormenor esplende.
Muralhas e crateras
o baço olhar não devassa.
Antes se embrulha em bruma
ou se molha nas espumas
sem chegar à medula.
Algemado ao óbvio, míope
nosso olhar impotente
não descasca o ovo da vida
nem colhe o sol em seu cerne.

The Precarious Gaze

The retina cannot reach
what is being woven out of sight.
Nor can touch imagine
what grows beyond the flesh.
Spectacles and magnifying glasses cannot
correct congenital blindness.
We always remain this side of
that fine line where the gold
of detail glistens.
A clouded gaze cannot penetrate
granite walls and craters.
Rather it is wrapped in mist
or soaked with spray
and never comes to the heart of things.
Chained to the obvious, myopic,
our impotent gaze
cannot peel the shell from life,
nor can it gather to its core the sun.

Ilusões

Ó ilusões, fantasias
neblina em pupilas
névoas contra vidros.

Embaçais o espelho.
O vulto do corpo
procuro e não vejo.

Por vós deixei
várias sandálias
sobre calçadas.

Por vós alcei-me
transviada no rumo
de andrômedas.

Asas abertas.

Illusions

Oh illusions, fantasies,
a misting of the eye,
clouds against the windowpane.

You fog the mirror.
I seek the body's outline
and do not see it.

For you I left
some sandals
on the sidewalk.

For you, I ascended
losing myself along the way
to those Andromedas.

Wings spread wide.

Chamas

Ano após ano
entre cantigas e risos
apagas velas acesas
plantadas sobre glacê.

Até o dia em que
te roubam da boca
o fôlego para o fogo.

É quando vento ignoto
(quem sabe o hálito de Deus?)
decide soprar de vez
a chama dentro de ti.

Flames

Year after year
amid songs and laughter
you blow out burning candles
planted on the icing of the cake.

Until the day
they steal the breath
straight from your mouth.

The day that unknown wind
(could it be the breath of God?)
decides to snuff out on the spot
the flame within you.

Velas ambíguas

Vida véspera da morte.
Poeira nos olhos
o esplendor da hora
disfarça o velório.
Ardem ambíguas
as chamas das velas.

Ambiguous Candles

Life, the very eve of death.
Dust in the eyes
the splendor of the hour
mask the last rites.
The candle's flame
flickers, ambiguous.

Sorveteria

Dia de verão qualquer
no labirinto dos *shoppings*
os homens tomam sorvete.

Alguns engolem vorazes
receosos de que o mormaço
lhes arrebate a porção.

Outros, lentos, não acertam
com o creme fugaz o ritmo
da fome. Morrem na fonte.

Poucos os que se deleitam
fruindo o açúcar e a neve
sem dúvidas sobre a dádiva.

Existe quem torça a cara
às iguarias servidas
imaginando outras raras.

E quem enfeite o bocado
de caldas extras, perfume
de licores, nozes finas.

Todos um dia qualquer
terão suas taças vazias
lábios imóveis, mãos frias.

Ice Cream Shop

On some summer day or other
in a labyrinthine mall
people are eating ice cream.

Some wolf it down
afraid the sultry mugginess
will wash it all away.

Others, lingering, do not adjust
their fleeting vanilla to the rhythm
of hunger. They die at the source.

Only a few take true delight
enjoying the sugar and the snow
devoid of doubts about the gift.

There are some who grimace
at the delicacies being served
imagining others rarer still.

And some who decorate it all
with bits of extra topping, scented
syrups, fine ground nuts.

All of them one of these days
will find their glasses empty
lips immobile, hands glazed.

Manaus outra vez

Lojas e mais lojas de ótica ao longo das ruas.
Em vão procuro lentes à prova de espaço e tempo.
Lentes que anulem distâncias soberanas, infinitas
e tragam até mim as límpidas imagens de antes.
Meus olhos se esforçam por desenterrar Manaus
vasto mercado sem teto, garagem a céu aberto.
Aqui e ali icebergs do neoclássico perfil:
a cúpula do teatro, o alto frontão de um palácio
mas lápides verticais logo interceptam a paisagem
e crua explosão de cores vem mascarar
as fachadas do sisudo casario vestido de cinza e limo.
Busco o discreto comércio, o recato da perdida
província onde se entrava por altas portas estreitas
pedindo a mercadoria a pessoa conhecida.
Tudo sem o menor escândalo, sem os escancarados
cartazes e os estridentes berros de alto-falantes.
Busco a quieta face oculta bem anterior ao caos
folias de Carnaval de três efêmeros dias
o aprazível recanto onde reinava um silêncio
rompido apenas por sinos e bondes sobre trilhos.
Nada do rugir selvagem do transitar incessante
nem da multidão anônima desfilando sem rosto.
Agora, mal avanço, carros tomaram as calçadas
e barracas acamparam carregadas de eletrônicos.
Estaco: a árdua persistência do verde me assombra:
vejo enfim fícus, oitis, mangueiras e mamoeiros.
Todos atestam o milagre, fruto das fecundas chuvas.
Anos a fora cresceram, porém ficaram baixotes
junto a imóveis manadas de exóticos elefantes.
Procuro em vão igarapés a fluir sob pontes
arrastando ribanceiras, galhos, troncos, folhas.
Não mais canoas, banzeiro, alagadas cuieiras
nem flutuantes, palafitas, touceiras de canarana.
Só mesmo infectos dejetos, poças gangrenas de lama,

Manaus Once Again

Store after store selling glasses along the streets.
I search in vain for glasses good against space and time.
Lenses to nullify the absolute sovereignty of distances
and bring to me clear images of the past.
My eyes struggle to disinter Manaus
from that vast roofless market, that open-air garage.
Here and there icebergs of neoclassical profile:
the theater's cupola, a palace's pediment,
but vertical slabs quickly block the view
and a raw explosion of color comes to mask
the facades of somber buildings dressed in aging grayish-green.
I look for a discreet shop, the reserve of the lost
province, where one entered through high and narrow doors
asking for merchandise from people whom one knew.
All without the slightest gaudiness, no blatant posters,
no loud-speakers and their strident bellowing.
I look for a quiet hidden face from long before this chaos
Carnival follies of just three fleeting days
the pleasant corner where there reigned a silence
broken only by the sound of bells and streetcars on their tracks.
None of the savage roar of endless traffic
nor of the anonymous crowd parading by without a face.
Now I can barely take a step, the sidewalks blocked by cars
and street stalls bursting with electronic implements.
I stop short: astonished by the tough tenacity
of green: at last I see *licania,* fig trees, mango and papaya.
They all proclaim the miracle, fruit of fertile rains.
For years they've grown, but stunted in the shadow of
those stationary herds of exotic elephants.
I look in vain for channels flowing under bridges
carrying along riverbanks, branches, trunks, leaves.
No longer canoes, rolling wakes, water-logged calabash,
nor floating shacks, houses on stilts, shoots of swamp grass.
Just malodorous debris, gangrenous pools of muck,

casebres de restos, folhas de zinco, escórias, miséria.
Das submersas, semi-extintas e humilhadas águas
somente um manto de mato denuncia-lhes a umidade.
Para rever a cidade, fecho os olhos.

Manaus, 2003

shacks made of scraps, zinc sheeting, dross and misery.
Of the submerged, almost extinct, humiliated waters,
only a cloak of underbrush reveals the hidden moisture.
To see the city once again, I shut my eyes.

Manaus, 2003

Das coisas

Algumas são perecíveis.
As comestíveis, por exemplo,
tão assimiláveis e semelhantes
nas urgências e desgastes do corpo
tão irmãs no destino decadente
mergulham conosco na voragem.

Outras são descartáveis
e se afastam de nós cada vez mais
rejeitadas por nossos gestos
rebaixadas a lixo e ainda assim
recicláveis com direito pleno
à metamorfose e reencarnação.

Grande parte das coisas
é de assombrosa resistência
matéria incólume pelas eras
muralhas e pirâmides de pedra,
pontes, arcos e torres de ferro,
coroas de ouro e diamante.

Efêmeros seres em trânsito,
devemos conviver com presenças
tão duradouras que até diríamos
participantes da eternidade.
Destas mantemos distância
devido às incompatíveis esferas.

Abro o guarda-roupa e encontro
os casacos com que meu filho
enfrentou a neve de Chicago
e caminhou ao sol da Califórnia
a camisa de um ido Carnaval.
Restos de seu rastro no mundo.

Of Things

Some are perishable.
Edibles, for example,
so easily assimilated and familiar
in their urgency and bodily deterioration,
brothers to our destiny of decay,
they plunge with us into the yawning gulf.

Others are disposable,
moving further and further from us
rejected by our gestures
reduced to garbage and even so
recyclables with all the rights
to metamorphosis and reincarnation.

Most things however
are of astonishing resistance
material safe from passing centuries
great walls and pyramids of stone
bridges, arches, and iron towers
crowns of gold and diamonds.

Transitory creatures on our way,
we have to live with presences
so durable we could even call them
participants in eternity.
From these we keep our distance
due to the incompatibility of our spheres.

I open the closet and find
the jackets in which my son
faced the snows of Chicago
and walked beneath the California sun
and a shirt of some past Carnival.
Signs of his passage through this world.

Não fosse a vida humana
assim breve, impermanente
poderia vesti-los a qualquer instante
perfeitos, embora pendurados
bem mais de uma dezena de anos
nos ombros fantasmas dos cabides.

Como disse um amigo às vésperas
de seu embarque definitivo:
o mundo só se acaba pra quem morre.
Daí a sobrevivência das coisas.
Apesar da aparência precária
da mudez e paralisia, resistem.

Longo é o circuito de tantas coisas
pequenas enquanto o tempo nos destrona
derrubando-nos ao rés-do-chão.

If human life were not
so brief, so fleeting,
he could put them on at any moment,
perfect still, although they've rested now
for more than a dozen years
on hangers with their ghostly shoulders.

As a friend said on the eve
of his definitive departure:
the world only ends for the one who dies.
Hence the survival of things.
Despite the precarious appearance of
muteness and paralysis, they persist.

Long is the cycle of so many little
things while time dethrones
and throws us to the ground.

Part Three:
Íntima fuligem / Intimate Soot

Véspera de violetas

"Já estou sentindo
As violetas crescerem sobre mim."
Murilo Mendes

Em qualquer das cenas
por onde quer que te movas
violetas sempre acenam
com a promessa do fim.

A vida é por um triz.

On the Eve of Violets

I can already feel
Violets growing over me.
Murilo Mendes

Wherever you go,
whatever the scene,
violets are always beckoning
with promise of an end.

Life hangs by a thread.

Walden

A velhice é pedra
no meio do caminho.

Cheguei tarde ao lago.
A noite me roubou
a cor das águas.

Pudesse eu ao menos
transpor o portal da lua
e na altura resplandecer.

Walden

Old age is a stone
in the middle of the road.

I reached the lake too late.
Night had robbed me
of the water's color.

If at least I could have
passed the portal of the moon
to glisten from those heights.

Adeus verde

Não tenho mais quintal.
Foi-se o da infância.

Ao alcance de meus braços
terra, orvalho, sons, insetos
bichos de pelo, penas, cascos
árvores de galhos vergados
mangas, goiabas, jambos, cajus.

Além da fartura das polpas
folhas que amáveis me abraçavam
afastando calor e luz.

Hoje se tenho sobre a mesa
uma bandeja com frutas
já me dou por contente.
Minha fome é bem pouca.

Os bichos sumiram todos
e a sombra, sempre presente,
transborda e me sufoca.

Good-bye Green

I no longer have a garden.
The one of childhood is gone.

Within reach of my arms
earth, dew, sounds, insects,
pets, feathers, shells,
trees with twisted boughs,
Mangos, guavas, *jambos,* cashews.

Beyond the richness of their pulp,
leaves like friends, embraced me,
banishing heat and light.

Today, if I have a tray
of fruit on the table
I feel content.
My hunger now is small.

The insects all have disappeared
and the shadows, always present,
now overflow and drown me.

O encontro

Deu-se em campo aberto
a léguas de qualquer baliza.
Apenas a figura nítida
recortada na neblina.
Coração latejando
em ritmo de passarinho
mal pude balbuciar:
Onde estavas, menino,
longe esse tempo todo?
Em que lugar do mundo?
Quem são teus amigos
agora e aquela paixão?

Em sutil delicadeza
com a fria ponta dos dedos
tocou-me de leve os lábios
e sorrindo matreiro disse:
É segredo, mãe. É segredo.
E mergulhou no nevoeiro.

Encounter

He appeared in an open field,
miles from any marker.
Just a clear-cut figure,
etched against the fog.
Heart pounding
like a bird's,
I could barely stammer:
Where have you been, my child,
all this time?
Where in the world?
Who are your friends now
and where is your passion?

With subtle delicacy,
with icy fingertips,
he touched me lightly on the lips,
and smiling slyly, said:
It's a secret, Mom. A secret.
And he sank into the mists.

Pequenas esperanças

Qualquer grande esperança é grande engano
Camões

Amanhã, queira Deus,
não seja o último dia.
Que ainda haja tempo
não pra inútil mala
mas pra despedidas
que o afeto pede
entrega de alguns presentes
acerto de questões práticas.
Que reste tempo hábil
pra deixar a casa em ordem
revisar armários gavetas
rasgar papéis sem valor.
Que a passagem seja rápida
e razoável a conta do hospital.

Small Hopes

Any great hope is a great deception.
Camões

Tomorrow, God willing,
won't be the last day.
May there still be time,
not for the useless suitcase,
but for the good-byes
that affection begs of us,
the giving of some presents,
the settling of practical affairs.
May there be time enough
to put the house in order,
look through the wardrobes and the drawers,
tear up meaningless paperwork.
May the passage be swift,
the hospital charges reasonable.

Retrato

Já viste pássaro
ter raízes?
Já viste árvore
ter asas?
Já viste peixe
ter voz?

Olha pra mim.

Portrait

Have you ever seen a bird
with roots?
Have you ever seen a tree
with wings?
Have you ever seen a fish
with a voice?

Look at me.

Vento

Só os auto suficientes
ou anestesiados loucos
torcem a cara ao vento
    rejeitando
o beijo da brisa
           no rosto
o invisível abraço
          no corpo.

Wind

Only the self-sufficient
or anesthetized madmen
twist their head away from the wind
    rejecting
the kiss of a breeze
                on the face
and on the body
                its invisible embrace.

Surpresa

Junto a mim, em plena rua
a multidão desmorona.

Dos velhos quintais da infância
Flavinha me surge alegre
com suas tranças de ouro
e vestido rosa organza.
Frente a nós um meio século
em puro milagre se eclipsa.

Falamos do instante presente
e do presente do instante.
Sorrimos leves, felizes
como se pulássemos corda
ou passeássemos de barco
no espelho do Rio Negro.

Surprise

Around me, in the middle of the street,
the crowd falls apart.

And from the backyards of childhood
Flavinha surges forth, filled with joy,
with her golden tresses,
and clothed in pink organza.
Before us, a half century lies
eclipsed in utter miracle.

We speak of the present moment
and of the presence of the moment.
We smile lightly, happy,
as if skipping rope
or on a boat ride
on the mirror of the Rio Negro.

A note on the author and translator

Astrid Cabral is a leading Brazilian poet and environmentalist who grew up in Manaus, on the Amazon River. She has won a dozen literary awards in Brazil and her work has been included in over sixty anthologies. Among her twenty books are the collections *Gazing Through Water, Cage, The Waiting Room, Word in the Spotlight,* and *Intimate Soot.* Her poems have appeared in over thirty magazines in the United States, including *Bitter Oleander, Catamaran, Cincinnati Review, Confrontation, Dirty Goat, Osiris, Per Contra,* and *Poetry East.* She is the translator of Thoreau's *Walden* into Portuguese. Her book *Cage,* Amazonian animal poems translated by Alexis Levitin, was released by Host Publications in 2008.

Alexis Levitin has published forty-seven books in translation, mostly poetry from Portugal, Brazil, and Ecuador. In addition to five books by Salgado Maranhão, his work includes translations of Clarice Lispector's *Soulstorm* and Eugénio de Andrade's *Forbidden Words,* both from New Directions, as well as Astrid Cabral's *Cage.* He has served as a Fulbright Lecturer at the Universities of Oporto and Coimbra, Portugal, the Catholic University in Guayaquil, Ecuador, and the Federal University of Santa Catarina, in Brazil and has held translation residencies at the Banff Center, Canada, the European Translators Collegium in Straelen, Germany (twice), and the Rockefeller Foundation Study Center in Bellagio, Italy.